Foghorns

Saved Lives, Too

Lighthouse Living
in Michigan's
Upper Peninsula

by
Vivian DeRusha Quantz

FOGHORNS SAVED LIVES, TOO
Lighthouse Living In Michigan's Upper Peninsula
By
Vivian DeRusha Quantz

Copyright © 1999
Keeper's Publishing
First Printing 1999

Published by: Keeper's Publishing
116 North Carlshend Road
Skandia, Michigan 49885
(906) 942-7875

Cover: Rebecca Parish

ISBN: 0-7392-0157-3

Printed in the USA by

MORRIS PUBLISHING
3212 East Highway 30 • Kearney, NE 68847 • 1-800-650-7888

Dedication

In loving memory of my beloved parents
Louis and Jessie DeRusha
and
With much love to
My fifteen brothers and sisters
and all our descendants

Acknowledgements

To my grandchildren, who gave me the incentive to share the history of my childhood with them.

Many thanks to my brother, Emmett, for reading my manuscript and along with sisters, Edna, Carol, Theresa and Jeanette, who all shared memories and critiqued where necessary.

My daughters, Beckie, Berty, Gigi, Georgia and Ruth, who encourage me by believing family and memories are important.

Tom Farnquist read my manuscript, liked it, and furnished the photographs for the cover.

The Great Lakes Shipwreck Historical Society of Sault Ste. Marie and Whitefish Point, Michigan, who have been so faithful in restoring my childhood home for all to enjoy. I am amazed at what has been accomplished.

I am grateful to the organization, Lightning Strike and Electric Shock Survivor's International, for helping me understand the devastation an electric shock or lightning strike can cause. With special thanks to the Florida Chapter for giving me the opportunity of being a help to others.

I've saved the best for last. My husband, Howard, thanks for giving me time, space and the encouragement to go on after the shock. Everything we've done for over forty years have been joint efforts.

Table of Contents

1

Journey to an Island

My father, First Assistant, Louis C. DeRusha began his lighthouse career at Detroit River Lighthouse in the early 1920's. He was ordered to Devil's Island in April of 1928.

"Dad was gone and we were all lonesome for him. It would be after school was out before we would see him again." Sister Edna, whom we called Teddy, sat in the big chair reminiscing about the move to Devil's Island, one of the Apostle Islands in Wisconsin.

The family, having been left behind to finish the school year and pack up to move, were to be ready when Dad returned for them.

"Most of the kids were apprehensive about moving. Not me." Teddy pointed to herself. "Mother always said I had a roving foot like Dad. I was always happy to move, see new places and make new friends."

Moving to an island out in Lake Superior conjured up all sorts of imaginations. Bears and wolves might be out there. They might get sick and die. Maybe they would run out of groceries and starve to death.

Letters from Dad didn't answer their questions. "Mother said we'd have to wait until Dad was ready to tell us, or wait until we were there to see for ourselves." Teddy liked the anticipation she was feeling. "I was so excited I could hardly sleep at night. I knew it would be a great adventure."

When Dad arrived the family was eager to leave. He bought a Packard car, loaded it with Mother, six of their children, one grandchild, said goodbye to friends and began the long journey to a place called Devil's Island.

The trip was long and tiring. "Mom had Emmett and Jay (Janiece) in the front seat with Dad. All the rest took turns sitting on the seat or on crates on the floor between the front and back seats. Louis, the grandchild, went from one to another, which ever could keep him quiet. Changing his diapers in that crowded car was quite an experience." Teddy held her nose remembering.

"We picnicked on the way, sang songs and tried to get some sleep. We were so glad when Dad stopped the car and said 'We're here.'"

"He meant we were in Bayfield." Edna continued. "It was still a long boat ride to the island where the lighthouse was. The boat that took us to the island was like a launch. When all nine of us, all the personal luggage, and the Captain, were in the boat it was only inches above the water. Even though the water was calm, the rocking of the boat made me sick. I threw up all the way out to the island." Teddy shook her head in distaste as she relived the journey.

During the summer months the family lived on the Island, occupying the house nearest the light tower, next to the Captain's quarters. The school year was spent in Bayfield in a house near the canning factory and lumber mill. The family cleaned many bushels of beans for the factory during the harvest months, and picked huge morels from around the lumber piles.

The highlight of the family's stay at Devil's Island was when the President of the United States visited the Island in the summer of 1928.

Teddy's memories continued as we shared a cup of coffee. "Mom was so disappointed, she was in the hospital in

Ashland and missed the President. We were all dressed in new clothes Mom sewed by hand for the occasion. Brother Emmett had a new bow tie and the girls' dresses were decorated with pretty ribbons. All five stood in line to greet President Coolidge and his wife with a bow and curtsies as they alighted from the boat. Secret Service men were all around, protecting the President. Everyone enjoyed the food from the laden picnic tables. Emmett, having helped himself to the chocolate cake, had his face cleaned, and the ribbons on my dress were retied by the first lady, Mrs. Coolidge."

Father's tour ended after my (Vivian) birth at St. Joseph's Hospital in Ashland in April of 1929. His transfer took us to Big Bay, Michigan.

Vivian DeRusha Quantz

A Night to Remember

Stannard Rock Lighthouse, located forty miles from Marquette, Michigan in the middle of Lake Superior, could be a dangerous place to be a lighthouse keeper. Dad was stationed there in the early 1930's. Storms on the lake could be ferocious. As a young child I remember my throat burning with fear while seeing the pain filled eyes of my mother during one of those storms. Cuddled in a blanket on the living room couch, I watched my family gather around the short wave radio. A hush hung in the room as we strained to hear through the static. While the storm raged outside I felt every clap of thunder jar my insides into jelly. Mr. Sormunen, new to the Stannard Rock crew, and Dad, left early in the day for the "Rock." Caught in a terrible storm they hadn't reached their destination.

The words, *lost, drowned, not coming home,* tumbled in my head. I closed my eyes to shut out the signs of panic.

"Dad will be all right. God will take care of him," my older sister Vi said. "God isn't out in this storm," her husband mumbled.

I waited for Mom to tell me everything would be all right. Her silence turned the knife of fear in my heart. Life without my father would be terrifying and empty. I sank into the corner of the couch heartbroken and afraid.

Many visited during the night, from the Marquette Lighthouse, the Coast Guard Station, and people from town. Some policemen stopped. Occasionally, when Dad stopped off at his favorite tavern after being at the Rock several weeks, he would need a little help up the hill to our house on the corner of Michigan and Pine streets. Our friendly policemen made sure he got home safely. This time they showed their concern with words of encouragement and sympathy.

All through the long night we waited. Lake Superior showed no mercy. The Coast Guard rescue team could not get out because of the high, angry seas. Mother broke her silence. "I will not give up. He is going to come home to us, you all just wait and see." If Mom believed Dad was alive, then I could hope too.

By morning the lake calmed enough so the Coast Guard crew could go out to search. Dad and Mr. Sormunen, clinging to the overturned boat, were rescued near Big Bay. I sat on the edge of the couch, listening to every bit of news. I saw in my mind the waves crashing and rolling in the fierce wind. I felt the bang and heard the crunch when a wave dropped the boat onto a reef, and I chilled in the icy water, as the men clung to the boat taking off their clothes, to stuff in the hole, trying desperately to keep the boat upright. I rode the tunnel made by a huge wave much like a surfer rides the inside of a great wave on the ocean, and came out on top with the wind and rain taking my breath away. Then being sucked below again, with nothing to do but cling desperately to the boat.

Wrapped in blankets Dad staggered into the room, exhausted and chilled to the bone. He had a stiff drink and for once Mother didn't say a word. Dad filled in the story concluding with, "The boat held together and we knew we were safe." I was thankful because I knew Dad could swim only enough to pass the service test!

Dad and Mr. Sormunen left almost immediately for the Rock. There were only two men there, and they needed help. I wanted my dad to stay home. The fear knot had begun to untie upon Dad's return. Now it was back. I would not leave my mom's side until Dad's voice came over the radio, and I knew he was safe, at Stannard Rock!

3

Moving to a Lighthouse

My third grade teacher knew I was sad. She gave me a shiny new dime to cheer me up. Third grade was over and I was moving away. I would miss her, my school, and my friends. Most of all, I'd miss Peter. I loved Peter. He gave me candy and carried my books.

Arriving home I found everything a mess. Furniture and boxes were everywhere.

"Where's my mom's picture off the desk?" I shouted.

"It's packed safely in the drawer," my sister Jay consoled me. Of my six older sisters, she was still at home.

"Run now, Sis, check your room. See if everything is ready to go. Harold is coming at six to load the moving van." Harold, my brother-in-law, was big with bushy black eyebrows. Sometimes I felt uneasy around him. He didn't like kids much.

Shouts from the movers echoed with my footsteps in the hallway upstairs. My room was empty except for mattresses on the floor. Harold would load them in the morning. I loved every corner of this room, even though I had to share it with two of my sisters. Knots tied my stomach tight. Dark murky blue was how I felt inside. With stinging eyes from holding back tears, I stopped in the doorway of my parent's room. The big chair by the fire-place where they read to us was gone. I'm scared. We'll never have another home like this, I thought. I wanted to crouch in a corner. Instead I went downstairs to find my family.

Next morning Mom woke us from the mattresses on the floor. She herded us to the bathroom where a quick swipe of a cold wet wash cloth brought us fully awake. "Hot chocolate and toast are on the kitchen table. Hurry now." Mom swiped the last face as she spoke.

I knew Mom was worried by the wrinkles around her eyes and the tightness of her mouth. Mom did not like changes, and moving to a lighthouse was a big one. I hoped she wouldn't let her temper loose or we'd be in for it. "Good morning, kids." Dad appeared in the kitchen doorway. "Everything is going along well, Jess. The van is packed. Time to get going." Dad's soft voice told me he recognized Mom's feelings.

We gathered around our new black Ford sedan in the cool, crisp air of the first week of June, 1937. The trunk door was finally shut. Blankets and pillows were piled on the back seat. We were to sit atop them.

"We'll bump our heads," said big brother Emmett. He was six years older than I was. In the car he sat behind Mother with five year old Wayne. Seven year old Theresa was next to me. Three year old Carol was in front with Mom and Dad.

Bumping along the gravel road, we felt every pothole. "Now I know why the ridges in the roads are called washboards." Emmett had his hand between the ceiling and his head. We bobbed like apples in a tub of water on Halloween. The young ones slept. The weight of Theresa's body added to my discomfort. Wayne stirred occasionally so Emmett could change positions. I suffered, hunched in the corner.

"There's a spring poking my backside." I complained to Emmett.

"Reach back and pull the blanket over it."

"I can't move."

"Give her a shove." Emmett was not sympathetic.

"She'll wake up and we'll have to play games with her. I'd rather suffer the torture," I grumbled.

We passed the town of Munising nestled on the shore of Lake Superior. I saw the beautiful curve of the beach. The fresh, cold smell of the blue-green water penetrated the car window. I breathed deeply. I loved the lake even when it was angry.

Part way up the Wetmore hill on the east side of Munising, Wayne screamed. It echoed in my head like a yodeler on a high mountain. Wayne's body stiffened as he rose out of the curve of Emmett's arm.

"Wayne, what's wrong with you?" Emmett's white face looked to me for help.

I reached for Wayne's legs. His screech tore at my ears.

"What am I supposed to do?" yelled Emmett.

"He's gonna die," my voice cracked with fear.

"What's the matter with him? Lou, Stop the car. Stop." Mom shouted over the noise, her face flushed with alarm. "Help him, Emmett."

Having sped up to reach the top of the hill, Dad braked. The car stopped suddenly on the side of the road. Theresa flew off the seat onto a box on the floor, with eyes wide open and a mouth ready to scream. "Don't you cry," I warned her.

Dad jerked open the back door, pulled Wayne into his arms, with Mom hands moving down Wayne's body. "His leg is asleep. We'll have to walk him," Mom said as she aided Dad to stand Wayne on his feet. Wayne continued to cry and scream as they walked him down the road. Emmett sat on the running board, cradling his head in his hands, totally exhausted.

The blue feelings were back. Anger churned inside me. The thought of leaving our nice home for a place at the end of a road somewhere was too much. I wanted to shout — to make Dad turn back. I was not going to be happy ever again.

Mom, Dad and Wayne returned quietly. We were on our way again. Wayne was in front, Theresa beside Emmett and Carol close to me. Carol was so cute. Her smile usually made me feel good, but not today. My stomach was in knots. We hadn't been told much about this move. Even though Dad was a lighthouse keeper on the Great Lakes, as long as I could remember the family had always lived in Marquette. This time we were to live at the station with him. I knew I wouldn't like it.

"Dad, tell us about this Whitefish place." I wanted to know what we were getting into.

"Whitefish Point is about thirty miles from where we turn off of this road," Dad explained. "The station is on a point of land. The lighthouse and coast guard stations are there, and houses to live in, but not much more."

"Is there a school?" Theresa asked. She liked school.

"There is a schoolhouse and a teacher. You'll be fine, Pumpkin." Dad knew Theresa was anxious about changes. She was small when she was born and had some catching up to do. I was scared she might die if she got too sick, and tried to be good to her most of the time.

Mom was quiet. I thought about what a good mom she was. She even sewed our underwear from flour and sugar sacks sold in stores. Some came in pretty colors, but there were times we wore "LITTLE JOE FLOUR" on our panties. Mom inspected us each morning to make sure the words didn't show through our clothes.

"Mom, are you gonna like living there?" I wanted her to be happy.

"It will be all right, Sis." Everyone called me Sis instead of Vivian. "The road into the Point will probably be muddy.

I'm concerned, but don't worry so much." I felt better when she smiled from the front seat.

The Whitefish Point Road looked good at first. Then the car began to feel as if it was sliding on grease.

"Wow, Dad!" Emmett said, resting his chin on the back of the front seat. "You're gonna have to stay awake. We're sliding all over the place. I hope we don't get stuck."

"You all be quiet back there," Mom ordered. She pushed Emmett's face back with her elbow. Recognizing the tone of her voice, we sat back and kept quiet.

Dad drove carefully. We lurched from side to side as the car slid in the muddy ruts. With my nose pressed to the window I was alarmed to see mud spattering all over the car. I was scared the moving van would run into us if we got stuck. Harold followed us closely all the way. Stretching to see out the back window, I nudged Emmett to look. The van swung back and forth so badly I was sure our stuff would be all broken up. Emmett patted my shoulder, telling me he understood.

The sun wasn't shining any more. The gray clouds looked like it might snow. "Will we ever get there?" Emmett mouthed the words I was thinking.

A horn blasted. Looking out the back window, we saw Harold out of the van, frantically waving his arms. "Stop! Stop!" We cried. The car slid to a stop. Dad stepped out, slid, and sat down hard in the mud! I burst into laughter. Emmett ducked out the car door. Mom said, "Oh my. Oh my," over and over. Pressing both hands over my mouth I struggled to get control. I'd be in real trouble if I didn't.

"The van is stuck," Dad announced. "We'll go ahead. It's about a mile farther. Removing his muddy coat, he slid into the drivers seat and started the car.

The government property sign was a welcome sight. "Thank God, we've finally arrived." Mom smiled.

In the near darkness, light shone from the windows of two white houses. We stepped out of the car into cold evening air. Our breath floated upward like white traveling clouds. I looked up, my head back as far as it would go. The lighthouse tower seemed to reach the sky. A beam of yellow light flashed in a circle.

The back door to the house which would become our home opened. "Hello, Mrs. DeRusha. Bring your children. Supper's ready," the smiling woman called.

The aroma of cabbage, carrots and onions set my mouth watering as I stepped into the kitchen. The blue feelings let up a little as the homemade soup warmed my tummy and made me sleepy.

Later, lying crosswise in the bed upstairs with Theresa and Carol, I thought about the trip and arrival at this new place. Snuggling under the covers I realized the knot in my stomach was still there. There were a million questions to be answered. Most of all I worried if we could make a home out of this place, like we had in our old house. Just before falling asleep I had a good thought. Mom and Dad are here. If anyone can make a home for us they can. I'll talk to them in the morning, I thought, as I slipped into sleep.

4

Foghorns Saved Lives, Too

Sitting straight up in bed I struggled to remember what had happened. A blast of sound bounced off the walls. I recognized the mournful sound of the foghorn. Like the high note of the musical scale, the WOOO held for five or six beats, dropping to the lowest note, before fading away until time to blast again.

The foghorn sound was not new to me, but this time the sound exploded like a fire bomb inside my head. Never had I been this close to a foghorn. A sailor, on a ship lost on Lake Superior, must experience this, I thought. I was wide awake. My imagination took me to the deck of a fog shrouded ship. Waves washed over the brow. Out of the darkness came the life saving sound of the Whitefish Point foghorn.

With my hands under my head I lay back staring at the ceiling. What an experience, I thought. What would it be like to climb up to the light? Would the height make me sick? How do you get up there anyway? Finding a way to the tower, where the light was, made me want to explore.

"Get up, girls. The movers want the beds." Mom called from the hallway.

Downstairs, I could hardly get through the mess to the kitchen. The movers were carrying our stuff in the front door while others were carrying stuff out the back. Harold was moving the other family out. No one noticed as I slipped out the door.

The blue water of Lake Superior sparkled on the other side of a sand dune. Soft sand dragging at my feet, I walked quickly past the brick building where the fog signal was. Reaching the top of the dune I caught my breath at the great expanse of water. Tiny waves, like riplets, kissed the sand and rocks of the beach. Overwhelmed, I stared. Inhaling the fresh breeze from the clear, blue-green water, my chest expanded like a balloon. I could look at the lake forever.

Scanning the beach to my left, I saw sparse trees on mountains of sand with green tufts of grass waving gently in the breeze. As far as I could see there were no people or buildings. On my right I spied the Coast Guard Station situated on a point of land not far away. I walked toward the white buildings and boats gleaming in the sun. The wet sand near the water's edge was easy to walk on. Flat, gray, flinty rocks were everywhere. Picking one up I felt the warm smoothness. I skipped it over the surface of the glassy water. Delighted, I skipped one after the other until my arm ached.

At the station, men in white uniforms hurried back and forth from building to boat to building. I stumbled onto a sidewalk reaching from the lighthouse to the station. Wondering how long I'd been gone I looked for the moving van. It was nowhere in sight. Looks like we're here to stay, I said to myself.

"Where have you been, Sis?" Dad asked. "Mom was getting worried."

"On the beach. The lake is so much bigger than at Marquette. I like the Coast Guard Station being close, too."

"Good for you! You'll be a big help with the little ones."

"I hope I don't have to have them with me all the time." I pouted. With a deep sigh I walked toward our new home.

The house was a duplex, split down the middle. We lived in the front and the second assistant's family lived in the back half. The buildings were in a line, with the fog signal building being nearest the lake. Next came the light tower attached to the house, on the second floor, by an enclosed walkway. Fartherest from the water the Captain's house sat; I thought the Captain should be nearest the lake to face trouble if it came.

"He's in position to lead us out if trouble comes. What do you expect, pirates?" Emmett tried to be patient with me.

"Pirates, or maybe prisoners." I remembered when prisoners escaped in Marquette and how scared I was.

"You're scared of everything. With your crazy ideas maybe you should write a book!" Emmett walked away disgusted.

"Maybe I will," I shouted at him. I wished he'd listen to me when I wanted to talk.

chapter

Rules and Responsibilities

Everyone pitched in to unpack and put things away. Many times I climbed the stairs carrying things to their destination. At last Mother was satisfied the house was presentable. One job assigned to me was to polish the staircase leading upstairs. This task was very important. Visitors to the lighthouse used the stairs to get into the tower where the light was. I learned to like the smell of linseed oil and turpentine.

There were rules that came with our new home. We couldn't go into the walkway to the tower. Dad kept putting me off each time I asked to go up to the light. I thought Dad made the rule just for me. I was wrong. The other family had the same rule. I could not take the young ones to the beach by myself. I loved it!

With permission I could go to the beach by myself. Emmett followed me one day. He untied and got into a row boat he'd left there earlier. "Come on, get in. we'll just go along shore," he promised.

"You'll go way out," I shook my head no.

"You just don't trust me. I promise I'll stay inside the pilings." Knowing I shouldn't I climbed into the boat. We skimmed between the pilings close to shore.

"Take me back, Emmett." I didn't think Mom would be happy with me. I should have asked permission.

"When I'm ready." Emmett's grin told me I was in trouble. We were out far enough, I knew the water was over my head.

"Emmett, take me back. I can't swim!"

"You're in a boat. What are you afraid of?" Emmett began to row the boat in circles. Fear burned my throat. Emmett rocked the boat. The spinning and rocking made me so sick and scared I put my head on my knees. With my arms holding my head down, I sank into myself until I felt like a small round ball. I prayed, *God, please make him stop.*

I unfolded myself when I heard the boat scrape the sand of the beach. Emmett had disappeared!

Shaking, I climbed from the boat. Sinking to my knees in the warm sand, I was unable to face my beloved lake. Something was different. I had been afraid for my dad before, but I loved the lake. In the spinning boat, through the fear, I became aware of the treachery the lake held for me by sensing the danger of taking it for granted. The lake was still beautiful, I would always want to spend time around it, but I would never feel entirely safe on it, ever again.

Emmett and I never talked about that experience and he was never aware of the fear that overcame me that day.

c h a p t e r

6

A Scream From Heaven

Exploring was my favorite pastime. Searching in the rocks for glassy swirls of color rewarded me with several beautiful agates. Making pictures out of white fleecy clouds passing overhead while lying on the warm sand was special. I could watch the young ones while Mom read, and daydream at the same time. Challenged by the height of the tallest sand dune in the area, I wanted to sneak away and climb it.

Excitement boiled like a soup pot in me one day when I was given permission to go to the beach alone. I was going to the dune! The excitement made me weak, but the fear of doing something I didn't have permission for, scared me.

Sand stuck to my sweaty body as I climbed. Water running down the dune had made a crevice in the sand. Using the tufts of grass to pull myself up helped, but sand kept dragging at me until I was exhausted. Considering the effort I thought I might quit, but inch by inch I kept on. Crawling on hands and knees I reached the top, sobbing with relief.

Sitting cross-legged like an Indian gazing into a fire, I scanned the scene before me. The expanse of Lake Superior, like a wavy mirror, reflected the cotton like clouds slithering across the sky. Nothing but water as far as I could see. Feeling so small, I felt my lips forming questions. *Who are you, God? If I died up here would you know? Would I go to*

21

heaven? Will I ever get across the lake to Canada? Lying on my back, my hands under my head, I closed my eyes.

A scream from heaven tore the breath from my body. Sitting up, something black scraped my back and shoulders. Flinging myself over the edge of the dune I stared into the beady eyes of the biggest hawk in the world as it passed over my head. Scared to death I slithered on my belly down the dune to the bottom. My heart pounded in my ears so hard I thought my head would explode. I ran through the trees until I remembered I was supposed to be at the beach. I turned toward the water.

After washing up and brushing off sand at the beach, I headed home, not knowing what to expect. I had been gone a long time. My racing mind tried to figure out what to tell Mom. Opening the screen door, I stepped inside.

"You've been gone a long time, Sis. Next time check in once in a while. Don't make your Mother worry." I couldn't believe my Dad didn't ask me where I'd been!

I returned to the dune one day. Looking up I was shocked to see a man. He had a big knapsack, and other things I couldn't see well enough to recognize. The dunes seemed to be a favorite place for hawks. They swooped low, then rose high to ride the breeze, soaring lazily about the blue sky. I learned the man was a naturalist. He trapped and tagged the hawks so their flight patterns could be studied. I wouldn't climb the dune again, but I was happy that someone else would enjoy the view. I just hoped he knew enough to keep his head protected.

7

Years Remembered

Whitefish Point Lighthouse Station became a wonderful home to me when I realized what a great place it was. Wonderful days of freedom, being able to roam the beaches, sand dunes and woods surrounding the Station, would not have been possible in Marquette. Mom and Dad were the same and my fears lessened.

There were lessons learned wherever I went and in whatever I saw around the area. For instance, searching for agates on the beach and determining what was real from the thousands of stones, was taught by Mother. I was told to wet the stone in the water, or in my mouth, to bring out the swirled colors. Thousands of rocks were discarded by her until I learned the distinguishing marks of an agate. Put into a jar with glycerine, the colors became bright. Placed on the table in the living room brought the dark wine colors of the couch and chair to life. Many visitors to the lighthouse were introduced to agate hunting by seeing the beautiful display in our living room.

Sand dunes were a pleasure to climb and roll down. Sliding down on a cardboard box was fun, too. There is a dangerous side to the dunes, also. The sands are constantly moving. If a dune has a cave like appearance it should be a sign of danger. The sand can move quickly. Learning to use caution when choosing a dune to play on was part of my education.

Because of the limited supply of friends, I learned to occupy myself with various things. I learned the various plants and flowers growing in the area. In the spring, arbutus was a favorite. The fresh sweet smell from a bouquet on the dining room table flowed through the house. Purple or yellow lady slippers were a bit more elusive, but priceless in beauty when found. There was a patch of what my mother called shing tang along the road near where our teacher, Mrs. Stevens, lived. This pink flower with deep burgundy specks smelled like sweet spices. Mother loved these flowers and treasured them as long as she could keep them in the house. I've never seen or smelled the likes of these since.

Many days went by without incident; however, boredom was never a question. Swinging high on the huge rope swing allowed me to see the lake over the trees and watch huge ships go by. Building sand castles, jumping rope, or playing hop scotch with my sisters, filled the days. Much time was spent simply feeling the breeze off the lake, watching the waves, or skipping rocks over the smooth surface. Life was great at Whitefish Point!

chapter

The Schoolhouse

A mile from the Lighthouse, along the road, the new schoolhouse was built. We watched each phase of the building process, knowing when it was finished we would be moving in. A foundation of posts in the ground and logs around the perimeter were the base. Men from the surrounding area, whose children would be using the facility, worked together with service men on the project. Although school started just after Labor Day, it was October before the building was ready to occupy. A bell tower rose above the roof. Four steps led into the small vestibule of the building. Upon opening the inside door, the teacher's desk could be seen at the front of the room facing the door, with a blackboard on the wall behind it. Three rows of desk chairs, four to a row, filled the center area of the room. A tall pot bellied, black stove stood midway near the right wall. A woodbox filled with kindling waited to be used.

Hooks lined the back wall on the left, placed to hold the student's coats. Below was space for galoshes, and other foot coverings worn in the winter. The right back wall was used for a small cupboard and a wood pile.

Two high windows in the front, one high window on the right side, and two regular windows on the left was the only light. The back door was located on the right side towards the back. The outside was painted white with a brownish trim.

The outhouse sat down a short path in the woods, used at recess and lunchtime.

School house at Whitefish Point
circa 1955

chapter

9

Lessons Learned in a One Room Schoolhouse

The long lazy days of summer were coming to an end. Theresa's curiosity was going to be satisfied. Mrs. Hawkins, the teacher, brought the students to order. The National Anthem was sung acappella and with gusto, and the Pledge of Allegiance recited in unison. School began in a house near the lake away from the Station.

Mrs. Hawkins explained forcefully that we were there to learn, respect our surroundings, and be kind to our fellow students. She would accept nothing less. I was happy because I liked to learn. It wasn't long before I learned what was expected of me! I was told I was to pass two grades in one year. It wasn't debatable. It scared me so bad. I was afraid because I wasn't sure I was smart enough, and I was scared because of what might happen to me if I didn't! Emmett accused me of being scared of everything. I guess he was right.

Although the school was from the first through the eighth grades, Mrs. Hawkins offered to teach Emmett and a local girl, Betty Becker, the ninth grade also. She was amazing to be able to do so much. We moved into the new one room school house after a few weeks. It was wonderful.

"There will be a program for your parents on Halloween. You will all have parts." Mrs. Hawkins announced the beginning of October. "You will all make your parents proud, won't you?" A chorus of voices answered, "Yes Ma'am!"

My poem was long and a little scary. Emmett bugged me, trying to confuse the words I was learning, but I memorized until I had it perfect. It was titled, "Me and Joe."

The school was packed. Every parent was there anxious that their child would do well. Emmett and Emily Borne were standing in the back. I finally knew how to get back at Emmett for all the times he wasn't nice to me! I went over it in my mind so I'd be ready. When my name was called I made my way to the front, took a deep breath and started my poem.

> *Emmett and Emily went out one night,*
> *Went out in his old flivver*
> *But when they remembered it was Halloween*
> *They both began to shiver*

I heard a loud laugh from Emily and I saw my brother's red face as he ducked out the back door. Everyone was laughing. I finished my poem without a hitch, sat down and burst into giggles. A stern look from Mrs. Hawkins helped calm me down.

During recesses we played tag and slid down the slide. Lunch times we hurried to eat and played games like Run Sheep Run, Tug of War, Hide and Go Seek, and many more.

The days of fall behind us, we found new things to do. We made a map on a large table. Rivers, mountains, farmland, gold, copper, and salt mines became real as we worked colors into papier-mâché and molded it to fit our assignments. We felt like artists as the world of rivers and mountains became real under our hands. We learned about so many things that first year at Whitefish Point.

I passed two grades that year. Mrs. Hawkins made it so interesting it was fun to learn. Emmett was nicer, too, after he learned I could fight back.

10

Visiting the Ancestors

The beautiful month of October, with a nip in the air and colorful leaves, told us snow would soon be falling. We took rides into the woods, breathing deeply to inhale the freshness, and allowing our eyes to drink in the beauty of the flaming colors. Dad turned west at Paradise on a road of ruts and sand. Traveling slowly we covered several miles before Dad stopped and announced, "We're here!" Out of the car, we gathered around him, wondering what "here" meant.

Like an Indian testing which way the wind blew, Dad put his index finger in his mouth, pulled it out, held it high in the air, pointed south and announced, "This is the direction, let's go!" He led the way through the woods. I never understood how the direction of the wind blowing could have anything to do with what direction we should go, but I had no trouble believing Dad knew what he was doing.

Single file Mom, Carol, Wayne, Theresa, and me, with big brother Emmett protecting us from the rear, anticipated the surprise Dad had in store for us. There was no way I could have imagined what I was about to see and experience. After hiking for a very long time Dad called a halt. "Listen," he commanded. I strained my ears. From a distance I heard an unmistakable roar. When Dad was assured we all heard it, he marched us through the woods once again. The roar grew louder. "It's water, Emmett. It must be a waterfall!" For once he agreed with me.

The deafening noise and the spectacular view of millions of gallons of golden bronze water thundering over the precipice of that giant falls took my breath away! I was enraptured by the wonder of the beauty around me. I strained to see where the wall of water landed many feet below. My mother screamed my name above the roar; unaware, I had moved too near the edge. Emmett grabbed hold of my shoulders. "Get back," he yelled in my ear. "You crazy, or something?"

We spent hours exploring. The Lower falls were as beautiful as the Upper Falls, but not so dangerous. I learned the name, Tahquamanon, but when Dad explained it meant Black Waters it became more real to me. Dad told stories of Indians, making me feel I was walking in the footsteps of my ancestors. He told of a little Indian princess finding a golden eagle and nursing it back to health. My imagination took me there, seeing the domed tepees and the simple way of life. Smoke from the campfire filled my nostrils and I saw the gestures of the Elders as they spoke to one another. I knew we belonged to each other even though years separated us. I wanted the day to go on forever.

In my imagination I returned to the area of the falls many times, dreaming of good times and hardships experienced by the People of the Woods, as I called them. My daydreams became so consuming my mother cautioned me to keep myself busy with other things. I was encouraged to read, and read I did, everything I could get my hands on. I traveled all over the world in my imagination as the words on paper allowed me to experience what the author was writing about. But I returned again and again to my life with the "Woods" people. Those trips back satisfied something deep inside me where nothing else touched me.

Another ride on another day took us to my parent's abandoned homestead. Nine miles west of Sheldrake near an old railroad line we sat on the sand in what used to be the front yard. Fallen logs from the walls and the door frame still standing were all that was left to remind Mom and Dad of a life gone by.

"We were happy here, Lou," Mom said. "Even though it was hard we were happy. So many things to remember, like the time your cousin visited." She was speaking to us now. "He was like an angel. A beautiful boy. Too beautiful for this world, I guess." Mom's voice drifted.

"Did he die?" Theresa asked.

"Yes, shortly after he went home. I knew it before anyone told us. A little bird fluttered at the window one day. It left when I recognized it was a messenger sent to let me know he had died."

"Who sent the messenger, Mom?" Theresa asked the question for all of us.

"God did. He does that because He sends peace along with the message. The bad news doesn't seem so bad if we know God cares enough to send a little bird to bring the news to us."

"Tell us about the fire. Was it bad? Was anyone burned?" We had heard it before, but when Mom was in the mood for story telling we were all ears.

"We smelled the smoke long before we thought there was any danger to us. Dad watched the wind direction closely. We hoped it would blow toward the lake and go out. It shifted several times so we couldn't be sure." My nostrils flared as she spoke. I heard the crackling of burning wood and felt the heat of the flames as my imagination took me back in time.

"When Dad was worried enough to tell us we had to leave, it was terrible. We packed all we could into the well.

Jeanette had a little piano she loved very much. She wanted to carry it, but we had so much we had to take we put it into the well hoping it would be safe until we returned. The fire was uncomfortably close when we headed out. Fire moves over ground quickly. We were lucky to get everyone out alive." Mom had a far away look as if she were reliving the rush to safety.

"The piano, is it still there?" Wayne headed for the over-grown well.

"There's nothing there, Son." Dad's voice was sad. "The fire took it all. Time to go, Jess."

Walking back to the car I felt the sadness of my parents. It must have been quite an adventure living way out here. My sisters and brother must have had a good time playing hide and seek, marbles and other games in amongst the tall trees. It was hard to think that my family had lived before I was born. It didn't seem right that I had missed out on all those family adventures.

We piled into the car ready to go home. Dad put the car in gear, stepped on the gas and the car buried its wheels in the loose sand. We pushed. Dad gunned the motor. Clunk! The axle broke. Dad's face turned red. He walked around the car, mumbling to himself.

"I'll have to walk out to get help. We're nine miles from Sheldrake, Jess. I'll go as fast as I can. You stay with the car." Turning to us he said sternly, "Stay close to your mother and behave yourselves."

"Take Emmett, we'll be all right." With a kiss for Mom and a wave to us, they left.

"What if it gets dark?" Carol was about to cry. I was silently worried about the same thing.

Mother spread a blanket in the shade of the car. Wayne, Theresa and Carol were soon taking naps. Mother sat with her back against a tree looking in the direction where Dad and Emmett had disappeared. I rummaged in the car for a book and settled down to read *Little Women* for the umpteenth time.

Late afternoon rays from a still warm sun dipped below the trees. A blast from the horn of a truck brought us all to our feet. Dad was back. The broken axle was fixed and we were on our way home again. I was so proud of my dad. He would take care of us no matter what. Of course, if Dad had listened to Mom and not backed into the loose sand, we wouldn't have had a broken axle at all. The relief on Mother's face told me what a strain she had been under. Just think, if Dad hadn't gotten back she would have had four scared, unhappy, hungry kids on her hands for the night. That thought made me appreciate her, too.

chapter

11

Rescue by Britches Buoy

Waves bruised the shore by the Coast Guard Station the morning Dad called for us to watch what was going on. A huge ore boat was anchored off shore. The Coast Guard launch rocked dangerously with each wave as they tried to reach the ore carrier.

"There's a woman aboard who needs to get to a hospital," Dad explained. "The sea is so rough the launch can't get close to the carrier, so they're going to try the britches buoy."

When the Coast Guard crew practiced maneuvers, I watched them work. I saw a sailor taken off a boat once. The weather was fine and there were no problems. The maneuver consisted of a contraption called a britches buoy, ropes and pullies. The pulley was attached to a pole on land. The britches buoy was made of a canvas like material shaped like a huge pair of shorts. Dad said some were built like a chair. This apparatus was attached front and back to the ropes forming a seat. The pulley was used to pull the seat out to the boat and then bring it back to the pole on shore. It worked slick and easy when the weather was beautiful and the lake calm.

The carrier was as close to shore as it could get without grounding itself. Sailors were running back and forth getting all the equipment needed. Dad left to see if there was any way he could help. Sitting on a cold rock on a knoll near the beach, I strained to see as much as possible.

35

When the ropes were secured to the pole on shore and to the pulley on the carrier, a sailor climbed into the britches buoy. The ropes began to unwind from the wheel they were attached to, and the buoy, with the sailor, began its journey to the carrier. Huge rolling waves kept the sailor above the water at times and under the water at times. I worried about the sick woman. How was she going to be able to ride the buoy across those high waves?

When the sailor reached the carrier, I ran home to get something to eat and talk to Mother about the woman. I gathered the woman was going to have a baby and something was terribly wrong. Of course, Mom never really said. We never talked about things like that.

Bundled in my winter coat, on the knoll, I saw the waves were still very high. There were two to worry about now; The woman and the baby had to be safe. I watched, waited and prayed. Seeing activity on the carrier around the britches buoy signaled the woman was ready to make her trip off the safe, warm ship. She must be terrified, I thought.

Leaving the carrier the buoy dipped into a huge wave, came up and dipped again and again. The woman's hands clenched around the ropes holding the buoy. Up and down the buoy made its way to shore. Sailors removed the woman from the buoy and quickly carried her to a waiting car. Her white face and straggly hair was all I saw as the car sped off, to meet the ambulance coming from the Soo, to take her to the hospital.

I worried until I heard the woman was all right. Emmett said if one day could pass without me worrying about something it would be a miracle.

chapter

12

My Brother Emmett

Emmett turned fifteen in August. Birthdays were special in our family. When Emmett saw the .22 caliber single shot rifle sister Viola gave him, all other presents faded into the background. He was so excited his face flushed and his hands trembled. The rifle was a dream come true. He had a .410 shotgun he used for birds, rabbits and squirrels, but now he could hunt big game.

The family was used to eating the small game Emmett brought home. He was a good hunter. At first he caught squirrels by chasing them into a twelve foot by four inch pipe he found in the woods, then hitting them when they poked their heads out. When the snow came he set snares for rabbits and our menu varied from squirrel to rabbit stew with an occasional meal of fried rabbit which was a family favorite.

Emmett would sneak along the trap line, his eyes searching for tiny holes where the soft, fresh snow had melted telling him something was hiding underneath. With his body bent over and every nerve alert, the snow pouffed as his hands swooped and came up with a partridge. There is nothing better than a platter of fried partridge to go along with the tales of the catch that Emmett could embellish so well.

One chilly October day Emmett left the house with his new .22 gauge rifle. He wandered west over the sand dunes. Having practiced shooting at cans and bottles he thought it was time to try his skill at a live rabbit or partridge. He walked like an Indian through the woods, carefully stepping over anything that would make noise. He was about to step into a small clearing when a white tail wagged in the air not fifteen feet ahead. Crouching so his leg steadied his right arm, he cocked and aimed at the yearling's head. He pulled the trigger, saw the ears of the deer twitch and its head come up, but it did not move and it certainly didn't fall down. Quietly he reloaded aimed and fired again. The deer continued to stand. He loaded, aimed and fired ten more times and the animal twitched and stood. By now sweat was pouring so hard down Emmett's forehead his eyes were stinging. The deer stood seemingly unafraid. Emmett loaded the thirteenth time, took aim, fired and the deer fell down dead. Having hunted with Dad many times Emmett knew he had to gut the animal, which he did. He was so weak from the excitement of getting his first deer, and the fear of it being illegal, he had a bad time getting home.

Mother turned from the stove when the back door banged. Emmett's white face scared her. "What's wrong, Emmett?" His teeth chattered so loud the room was filled with the sound. The rifle banged against his leg as his body seemed to be shaking to pieces. He couldn't speak.

"Go get your Dad." Mom yelled. Theresa dropped the dish towel on her way out the door.

Mother carefully took the gun from Emmett and guided him to a chair. "Did you shoot somebody, Son?" Emmett's head shook from side to side. "Thank God." Mom sighed with relief.

Emmett's hands gripped his knees so hard his knuckles seemed to pop out of the skin. Slowly he gained control of his breathing. As Dad came in the door Emmett said, "I killed a deer." Dad looked at him and burst out laughing. "It's buck fever."

"It's out of season, Lou. What are you going to do?"

"We'll bring it in. We can't leave it in the woods, it's not right."

"It's not right to have killed it either," Mom was worried. We were on government property and it was a risk to have out of season venison in the house.

Dad and Emmett returned after dark with gunny sacks full of venison. Mom cooked the meat in large pots with plenty of onions to cover the wild smell. We packed jars full of the hot meat, filled the canners and preserved the booty for future use. Emmett talked through it all until we knew the story by heart. He was so excited about shooting his first deer, wasting twelve shells didn't bother him a bit.

Our menu varied when Emmett wanted to fish. Dad bartered for a gill net, taught Emmett how to mend it, and set him free to do his thing.

There were pilings and wharfs protruding into the lake. Emmett found a place where the current caused an eddy between the pilings. With my help from the shore, Emmett carefully strung the net and anchored it where the swift water flowed. And he caught fish! — whitefish, trout and lots of herring. Helping Emmett remove those slippery fish from that net, especially when they were still alive, caused both of us to double up with laughter more than once. Dad gave Emmett a small galvanized smoker where he learned the skill of smoking fish. He found the best wood, kept the fire so there was no flame, the smoke was just right, and cooked those fish to perfection.

When Emmett was old enough he joined the Civilian Conservation Corps. He was stationed at Camp 3626 at Germfask. I missed him. Even though we kidded and competed with each other he was not only my brother, but my close friend. After he left I realized how important he was in my life.

The C.C.C.'s built roads and bridges. They made fire lanes through the woods and when the need arose they fought forest fires. The family was very proud of Emmett. He was a good man, took care of himself, worked well, and got along with everyone. Emmett joined the Navy, and served on LST 197 during the second world war. He married a girl from Richmond, Virginia, retired after the war, and returned to the Upper Peninsula for visits over the years.

13

Priestly Visits and Gospel Meetings

Mrs. Hawkins played the guitar. I heard there would be a Gospel meeting at the Coast Guard Station. Because I loved music and was curious to know what a Gospel Meeting was I wanted to go. Being Catholic, my parents said "No." Knowing anything to do with the Gospel had to do with Jesus I was indignant that I couldn't be a part of what I was sure would be a great time.

The evening came. We were warned to stay away from the Coast Guard Station. I sat on a log at the edge of the lighthouse property, as near to the meeting as possible, without disobeying.

The music wafted in the air. I could make out old hymns, *"The Old Rugged Cross," "Trust and Obey," "Faith of Our Fathers"* and others I knew. I felt I was a part of what was going on in that meeting, even though I couldn't be there. It took me a very long time to understand and forgive my parents for not letting me attend.

Some of the understanding came when my Dad got a priest to come to Whitefish Point. He came every three months and stayed at our house. He seemed so old. With a long white beard he scared us. We were so good for the couple of days we had him in our house. He held Mass in the Captain's living room.

I hated going to confession. There was no confessional. I had to kneel at his knee and confess the terrible things I had done. One time I confessed to a particular sin. He asked me a question about it. Fear tied my tongue so tight I couldn't answer. Sunday morning the Priest passed me without giving me the communion wafer. I thought I was going straight to hell. For days I was afraid to go to sleep for fear I would never wake up and would have to face the terrible wrath of God. If the Priest could read my mind like I believed, he would know how terrible I felt about breaking Mother's vase and hiding it in the living room couch. God and I were all right again when I remembered He was the one who died for my sins. When I brought the pieces to Mom I learned she had gotten it from a carnival and wasn't upset.

Mom wasn't too pleased with the good Father either. He always asked for blackberry juice with his meals. Mom would have to strain her canned blackberries to satisfy him. We wound up with dry blackberry cobbler because Mom wasn't about to waste anything.

The Gospel meetings were sure a lot more fun to listen to than the sober, sometimes frightening, Mass we had to attend. Because of the influence of those meetings I began to lose the paralyzing fear of God that made me picture him on a huge golden throne, with a golden baton, ready to smack me over the head. I believed He made me, He loved me and always would, no matter how I behaved.

c h a p t e r

14

Christmas

I awoke on Christmas morning full of anticipation. Emmett and I had hinted for months for the presents we wanted. I sat on the floor, near the beautifully decorated tree, in the corner of the dining room. The silver service I had polished the day before shone on the sideboard. A small wooden keg sat on a miniature stand in between the silver. A small glass held the burgundy wine that dripped from the tiny spout. Dad was never able to stop the tiny drops from falling. He would drink the catch sometime during the day and replace the glass to catch more falling drops.

A long thin package stood behind the tree, so tall it nearly reached the ceiling. There was only one. I couldn't quite give up the idea that there wasn't one for me too. My parents were surely playing a trick on me. I waited for the family to gather to open presents.

Carol and Theresa were given packages the same size and shape as mine. They tore at the shiny wrappings. Slowly I removed the paper, opened the cover of my box, and saw the face of my very pretty doll. My heart was in my toes as I thanked Mom and Dad for the gift. Emmett was handed the long package from behind the tree. The skis were dark wood with a lever to tighten the binders on his feet. They were beautiful. I finally had to admit to myself I wasn't getting skis. I felt kind of dead inside.

A gusty wind was blowing the falling snow as Dad left the house shortly after breakfast. We went about our chores. The huge turkey was stuffed, vegetables peeled, and pies were in the oven, before I could get away to my room. Lying on the bed I turned my face to the wall and gratefully fell asleep.

Theresa woke me. Dad hadn't returned and everyone was worried. The storm had worsened. Snow was drifting around the Lighthouse buildings. Wonderful odors from the kitchen filled the room, but my heart was heavy. What a Christmas, I thought. Mother opened a package which had arrived a few days before. Chocolate, smooth and sweet, melted in my mouth from the small pile Mother cut from the block sent from my sisters, Jay and Teddy. For the moment I almost forgot how sad I was. Remembering a package I hadn't opened I tore the paper off to find several wonderful books. Jay and Teddy had remembered my favorite pastime. If I couldn't have skis I could travel the world and forget. I loved the gift.

"The turkey is done," Mom announced.

A hearty "HO! HO! HO!" came from the suddenly opened door. Dad was home! He handed me a pair of skis.

"Here, Sis these are for you. Merry Christmas!"

My Dad had left our warm cozy home on Christmas day to find a pair of skis for me. He searched until he found a man who had a pair on a sled that he was willing to remove. They cut leather straps and attached them to the skis for my feet to fit into. Dad braved the storm through the drifting snow to make his young daughter happy on Christmas!

The sand dunes became the high light of the winter months as Emmett and I skied day after day. He was brave. Plummeting off the top of the highest dune, he sailed off the jump he cut into the snow. I couldn't bring myself to go to the top so Emmett cut a shelf about half way up for me

44

to start from. I flew off the jump, sometimes losing a ski, tumbling head over heels to the bottom, only to get up and ski again. I loved every minute of the cold biting snow in my face and the thrill of flying through the air. Dad came out occasionally to see what we were doing. Emmett tried to coax him onto the ski hill but he declined. We knew his pleasure came from seeing us so happy.

chapter

15

One Ugly Animal

Dad came into the kitchen, grabbed the broom and rushed out the door, calling for us to follow.

"Stay over there, and stand still."

"What's going on, Dad?" Emmett yelled, as he took my hand and ran to the place Dad told us to stand.

There was a space without trees to the west of the Coast Guard Station on the bay side of the lake. We stood in the clearing wondering and waiting to see what was going on. Men were shouting and making noise in the woods in front of us. Voices calling, "To the left. To the right. There he is. Watch him. Watch out," rang through the woods. One man, on the road, leaped from side to side peering though the trees.

Half scared I yelled at Emmett, "What is it, Emmett? Can you see anything?"

"Trees, I can see trees, that's all." Emmett stretched his neck, then ducked to see under the trees, but saw nothing. "I can't make anything out. We'll have to wait."

A layer of melting snow covering the ground made a squishy sound from trampling boots. Excitement rose as the shouts came nearer to the clearing.

"It's a big buck," Emmett shouted as a huge dark animal plunged out of the woods. "No it's not." Emmett almost whispered.

The animal ran toward us, spotted us, and came to an uncertain stop, looking back and forth as if deciding how to

escape. The frightened eyes were wide open, with a glint showing his fear. Slobber from his square, oblong jaw spilled onto the ground. A rack of horns, flat and curved on the edges sat upon his huge head. His body trembled, shoulders heaving from deep breaths, while snorting into the air. Hoofs as big as a man's foot pawed the ground sending snow up to his chin.

The woods were quiet. Men stood in amazement. Dad carefully circled the clearing until he was beside us.

"It's a moose." He said quietly. "He came over on the ice. He was spotted out there a while back. Everyone thought he'd be dead by now. It's from Canada. Never thought I'd see one here."

"What's going to happen to it, Dad?" Emmett's voice was as quiet as Dad's.

"We'll let it go. The authorities will be notified and will look after things."

"All right now, we've seen enough," someone shouted. "Let it go." The men faded into the woods circling toward the road.

Looking from left to right the moose turned. With a sudden lurch it disappeared into the trees. For a moment his hoofs could be heard. Then he was gone, leaving his prints in the snow, to remind us of having seen one of the most wonderful, ugliest animals in the world.

48

16

Carol's Mumps and Unsettling Rumors

The Saturday before Easter I was awakened early. We were going to Marquette to spend the holiday. All the packing had been done the night before except for toothbrushes. I was setting the table for breakfast when Carol came downstairs.

"Oh! No! Lou come here." Unbelief sounded in Mother's voice.

"It's mumps all right. No trip today," Dad announced.

What a crushing blow. Excitement at seeing my sisters and the probability of seeing a movie flew out the window. I inspected Carol, hoping to see a miracle, but her cheeks looked like a giant squirrel, with its cheeks full of nuts, looking for a place to hide.

"You did this on purpose." Theresa was indignant.

"That's ridiculous. You all watch your mouths." Mom tried to ward off more trouble for Carol.

Wayne came to her defense. "No one gets mumps on purpose. I'll probably get them, too." He didn't look too happy.

"It's not funny. When I had them it hurt to eat. Maybe you should go to bed, Carol." I wanted to get alone so I could sort out my feelings of disappointment.

So the trip was called off. The Easter Bunny would have to come to Whitefish after all.

Dad had hinted there was a special reason we were going to Marquette. He had something to tell the family. The secret tore my insides up until I couldn't stand it. At supper I asked, "What's the secret you were going to tell us in Marquette, Dad? I'm so excited."

Looks were exchanged between Mom and Dad. There was a very long pause. I wasn't sure I wanted to hear this after all.

"Well, there is bad news and good news. I'll start with the bad. There are rumors that the Lighthouse Service will be taken over by the Coast Guard. So I will probably have to retire."

Everyone began to talk at once, except me. I froze. Time stood still. The voices around me faded and I began to experience fear again. Whitefish Point was the most wonderful place in the world. I pushed away from the table to get away.

"Sit down, Sis," Dad said quietly. I slumped into the chair.

"We know this news is a blow to you. But we just have to deal with it. The good news is we won't have to leave while school is on. Maybe not until after next year.

"Where will we go, Dad?" Wayne acted as though this would be a great adventure. I hated him for not feeling bad.

"We'll start looking for a place. Maybe to buy. Where that will be, we don't know yet."

"May I be excused?" Dad nodded his head and I took off to the attic room where Emmett used to sleep. I was angry at him for not being there for me to talk to. I sat cross-legged before the window trying to sort things out. The pain was real, the fear was real. How could I deal with this all by myself? I felt someone sit on the floor beside me and a hand slip into mine. "I feel bad, too," Theresa said. We sat together for a long time. Mom called for us to come down. We felt better after having a few pieces of chocolate from the big bar. Many times when things went wrong, Mom helped us through with such a treat. Jay and Teddy were sure smart to have sent such a huge bar of chocolate.

Vivian DeRusha Quantz

c h a p t e r

17

Summer of 1938

Rumors continued to keep my family unsettled. Tempers rocked the family scene. Mother liked Whitefish and discussions of where to move and what to do usually ended in an argument. Mom was a homemaker. To disrupt her home became a major catastrophe. Emmett was home from Marquette, where he had been working, when things came to a head. Mom and Dad talked of breaking up. Sitting on the cellar door Emmett and I discussed the situation.

"Who will you go with, if you have to choose?" I asked.

"I'm not concerned who I'd go with, Sis. I'm not around much, but who would you go with?"

"I'd stay with Mom. I wouldn't have as much fun, but I couldn't leave her."

"This talk is crazy." Emmett shook his head. "It's not going to happen. Let's go skip rocks."

The conversation ended and the subject never came up again. Emmett was right. Things calmed down and returned to normal.

With Emmett gone things weren't the same. Theresa and I had became better friends, but her interests were more on the safe side, like playing hop scotch and jacks. I was the adventurous one, and without Emmett to find the escapades I was lonely.

There was a curve in the road between Whitefish and Sheldrake called the Horseshoe. During blueberry season a buyer's tent was set up there where pickers brought their berries to sell.

On Dad's days off we piled into the car with our shiny pails, a basket full of lunch and a huge thermos of kool-ade. Turning right at the Horseshoe we traveled the dusty sand road until Dad spotted blueberries.

Parking off the road under a shady maple tree we spread our much used Indian blanket. Mother was in charge of the lunch. Skipper, our pet terrier, stayed with her as usual.

Each grabbed a pail and ran to get our own spot on the plains where the berries were plentiful. Some were eaten, but we were soon satisfied and settled down to pick in earnest. I listened for Dad's call to lunch when thirst and hunger turned my mind from daydreaming to a break under the cool green leaves of the shade tree.

Dad always picked into a large blue speckled pail and after lunch and a short rest, wandered away to hunt the freshest, bluest berries he was always able to find.

The afternoon sun told us it would soon be time to pack up and head for home. We heard Mother calling for Skipper wondering where he had strayed to. We gathered around Mother. She was worried, it wasn't like Skipper to leave Mother alone. We called his name and looked as far as our eyes could see. He came toward us from the edge of the woods. He was running fast. We were so glad to see him, but he didn't come to us. He circled us racing as fast as his short legs would go, barking and circling, as if to move us closer to Mother. Skipper circled several more times, barking in short sharp yelps. Suddenly he headed toward the woods and disappeared out of sight. It was a mystery.

We called and called. Dad returned, concerned by the barking and calling. He stopped us from searching the woods for Skipper. The sun was setting when Dad insisted we leave for home. We were bewildered and in tears. We loved our pet. It was hard to leave without him.

Dad let the Coast Guard and the fishermen in the area know what had happened. He asked everyone to look out for Skipper. Two weeks later a man from the C.C.C.'s at Camp 33 sent word that a dog was at the camp and might be ours. Dad went to the camp and returned with a very tired, bedraggled Skipper. We cried again, this time with joy.

The C.C.C. officer told Dad there were bear sightings in the area where Skipper had gone into the woods. Skipper was a hero! We knew he had protected us from harm on that scary berry picking day.

We picked for days until Mother had canned enough for winter. Then we sold to the buyer until the season was over. Mother used the money to order from the catalogue what we needed for school, especially snowsuits and overshoes to brave the snow in, as we walked to school during the winter.

Mother called the summer the year of the company. It seemed everyone visited. Aunt Jane came. Uncle Ernie, Mother's brother, his wife Aunt Alice, and their two girls spent some time with us. Auntie and Uncle sang together, and without music. Beautiful hymns and lovely love songs wafted through the air as they stood face to face, hands entwined and faces aglow.

Cousins from the Rexton area visited. At times our home overflowed. It seemed everyone wanted to visit us at Whitefish before we had to leave. I was always excited when someone came, but the visit I enjoyed most was sister Teddy, her husband Bill and Bobby, my nephew. He was about a year old and was so cute. His hair was blond with a little curl which fell onto his forehead. Having him around took my mind off the awful rumors. We didn't know if we would have to move before school started and the summer was going so fast the knot of fear was growing by leaps and bounds.

Jay was visiting the night of the terrible storm. Mother was always nervous when storms came, so we were usually awakened and brought downstairs. Wind was howling making the windows rattle. Rain came down so hard it sounded like rocks pelting the house. Lightning brightened the room periodically and the thunder made me want to cover my ears.

Dad left the house for the fog signal. Mother walked the floor with her rosary. Jay did her best to keep Carol quiet. Storms never bothered Wayne so he was trying to frighten Theresa with stories of lightning strikes and house burnings. I liked to stand at the window and watch the storm, but Mother wouldn't hear of it, so I sat in the big chair wishing I could go back to bed. I fell asleep. It was light outside when I woke. The storm was over. From the window I saw an amazing sight. There were ships all over the water. They had pulled into the bay to escape the storm. There was one that was so high in the front it seemed to reach the sky. It flew a flag. I could see it was not the Stars and Stripes. Gleaming white reflected the early morning sun. It was close enough to see a uniformed man standing at the rail. I was sure it was the Captain. Up the stairs I rushed to dress, then out the door I flew to get a closer look. Dad was standing on the steps of the fog signal building looking at the ships. Running up the steps I shouted, "What is it, Dad?"

"It's a Norwegian ship. Going to Duluth. Something important going on there. I knew it was coming, but thought it would go by during the night. Quite a sight, isn't it Sis? I'm glad you had a chance to see it."

Slowly the ships left the Point. I watched until they all disappeared. I was thankful for the Lighthouse once again. What would have happened without the fog signal and light from Whitefish Point? My imagination didn't want to go there.

The swing was in a wooded spot to the west of the buildings. At times, when questions filled my mind, I headed for the swing, hoping to be alone for a while. Things were changing too fast. It seemed like every time good news came there was bad news to follow. We were to be able to complete another year of school before we had to move, but Mrs. Hawkins was not going to teach again. Mrs. Stevens, wife of a Coast Guard man, was taking her place. I was trying to get my mind used to the idea when the Captain's daughter and Carol shouted at me to get off. They began fighting about who was to get the swing. Trying to help, I suggested they take turns and I would push so they could swing high. Taking two small twigs of different sizes I said the longest twig picked would swing first and I would push twenty times each. They agreed. Carol picked the winner, climbed on the swing and I began to push. The Captain's daughter, insisted the swing was her's and she wanted it. I tried to tell her it was almost time for her turn when she ran toward the houses screaming. She returned immediately with the Captain. He had a butcher knife in his hand and angrily sawed at the rope until the swing was ruined. I wondered if there would ever be happiness at Whitefish Point again.

chapter

18

Relatives

Two graves lay side by side on a gently sloped mound inside the Gros Cap cemetery. A six by six inch four-sided wooden fixture rose from the earth to a height of about five feet. The inside was hollow except where a small door was located near the top. The door opened into a tiny room. Faded white paint covered the structure except for the edges which were painted black. My father placed bread and corn in the opening explaining the food was for the spirit journey of our Grandfather and Grandmother into the other world. The connection to my ancestors reminded me of the woods people of my imaginative journeys. Feelings of peace and security surrounded me. I belonged to the past and to the future, therefore I was whole.

Trips taken to St. Ignace, Rexton and Sault Ste. Marie were a wonderful part of my young life. Aunt Jane Goudreau met us at the door of the home she called "Manitou." Always a kettle of pea soup simmered on the stove when we arrived and Dad ate soup and johnny cake to please her as much as himself. She told wonderful stories of our ancestors. I heard about my Great Grandfather coming from France into Canada, marrying an Indian princess, then migrating to the States. My grandmother was also part Indian. My heart feelings were legitimate. I belonged to the land and had an Indian heart. There were hours of stories and the laughter rang in that little house as

Aunt Jane smoked her corncob pipe, slapped her thigh and occasionally stood to do a jig, right there in front of everyone. I was allowed to go up the ladder stairs to the attic where a skeleton hung from the ceiling. I was told it was an Indian ancestor. I was never quite sure of that, but it fit into my imagination perfectly. Aunt Jane's collection of old coins on a table under glass was so interesting I wanted to feel them, but didn't dare. Aunt Jane loved people. I think she loved my Dad most of all. The love and respect between them was unmistakable.

At Rexton we visited Uncle Jesse and Aunt Bid Derusha. We played from morning till night with many cousins, ate great plates of wonderful food, and when evening came we sat quietly listening to mouth organ and fiddle music until we were carried off to a huge room with several beds. We went to sleep in a bed and woke up on a mattress on the floor. It took a long time to figure out the mattress, with us on it, was moved during the night.

Visiting the Soo (Sault Ste. Marie) was just as exciting. Aunt Lavinia and Uncle Charles Paquin opened their home and hearts. They owned the Belvedere Hotel and Ship's Tavern. My cousin Emil tended bar there. The brass rail seemed very long and the brass spittoons were interesting until I was told what they were used for. Cousin Emil could make music anywhere and with anything. He wasn't shy about demonstrating, either. He once played a tune on a thimble. It was impressive!

Tales of family escapades and adventures were such a part of our lives. Roots and respect went deep into my soul and molded me as I grew. The courage of my great grandparents, the adventures of my grandparents and the humor with which my parents, aunts and uncles related the stories will be in my memory forever.

chapter

19

Same School Different Teacher

"I am Mrs. Stevens." Her brilliant blue eyes sparkled. Red hair, pulled back with a large tortoise clasp, framed her beautiful face. Dad had told us she was Irish, warned she might have a temper, and told us to behave. School was open and I was eager to have something new to think about.

The days went by without crisis. We behaved, learned, and enjoyed the camaraderie of our fellow students. We worked hard, played hard, and when called on to perform we did our best. The Christmas play was the highlight of the year. Mary and Joseph, the shepherds, and wise men all in homemade costumes turned our one room school house into the town of Bethlehem. Children representing the different families of the area including the Huttons, Hawkins, Bornes, and others, made their parents proud. I admired Mrs. Stevens. How she could get everyone to work together to put on such a beautiful performance was magic.

Things at the Point were better. Everyone seemed to have accepted the inevitable changes. My Dad, because of his age, would have to retire from the service. Others would be taken into the Coast Guard. When I begged Mom and Dad to stay at Whitefish they said "No." Dad had to go where he could find work. He would have a pension, but not enough to support a family. I was glad for school, and when I realized I would be going to junior high school the next year, I worked hard.

As the snow began to melt and the days became warmer I visited all my favorite places as often as I could. My passion for books had lessened to the extent that I hardly read except to do my school work. I grew moody and got in trouble with Mom for sassing. I knew she understood why I acted the way I did, but it didn't seem she knew how to help me. Maybe because she was having some of the same feelings.

The day school was over, and Mrs. Stevens handed me my certificate for entry into seventh grade, would have been the worst day of my life, except for the card Mrs. Stevens made for me. It said she was proud of me for all my hard work during a difficult time. She wrote, I know you will always do your best. It was the words, "proud of you" that really helped me.

chapter

20

Christmas With Friends

The tree stood in the left corner of the dining room waiting to be decorated. Open boxes of trimmings, collected and saved over the years, were ready to be hung on the pine smelling branches. One by one each child chose an ornament and handed it to Dad for hanging in the right place. Then we children sat back and watched the transformation take place. Garlands and tinsel shivered, reflecting the lights in the room. The night was special. Usually the trimming took place after we were in bed.

Wonderful odors of chocolate and cinnamon hung in the room making my mouth water for a taste. Cookies baked while Mother prepared a table with her special silver and cake plates. She was getting ready for a party. Excitement danced in the air.

Hearing what sounded like singing I ran to the dining room window. Hands cupped around my eyes to shut out the light in the room, I stared into the darkness. Several people stood in the snow. They sang from booklets held in gloved hands. We pushed at the window to see what was going on. Mom and Dad stood at the opened back door to hear better and greet the carolers. Wonderful hymns of Christmas, *"Away in a Manger," "Oh, Little Town Of Bethlehem," "Silent Night,"* and *"We Three Kings of Orient Are,"* sung in harmony, faded as the carolers moved from house to house so all could enjoy the gift brought to us from friends.

Everyone came in out of the cold to enjoy Mother's treats. Mrs. Hawkin's guitar was fetched. The harmonica was brought out and Christmas Eve was celebrated by family and friends.

After Theresa and Carol were asleep, I sat in my warm flannel pajamas at the top of the stairs listening to the music, dancing, and story telling going on downstairs. I was sure Jesus would be happy with the way his birthday was being celebrated.

chapter

21

Where to Now?

A cold wind blew off the lake. Waves bounded onto the beach splashing foam into the air. I was cold. Bundled into my winter coat, I found refuge in a crevice of a sand dune facing the water. Feeling physically sick, my knees pulled up to my chest, I tried to push out thoughts that seemed to bang the walls of my mind. Impossible for me to accept was the announcement from Mom and Dad. A piece of property had been purchased at Newberry. How could they do this? How could they think we could live happily away from the lake? I'll go live with Teddy or Jay, or anyone who would take me, as long as they lived by the water. I was so angry I thought I'd walk right into the lake and disappear.

Dad's voice penetrated my confused brain. "Pretty cold out here, Sis."

"I'm not cold," I lied.

Dad sat in the sand beside me, tucking a blanket around us both.

"Sis, you've got to understand what's going on here. We're all disappointed about these changes. We've got to think of Mother. She wants to try farming for a while. Her family were farmers, remember."

I slumped deeper into the dune. I knew a lecture was coming.

"Mother's life hasn't been easy all these years. Way back when we were at Vermillion, we were the only family there. There have been many heartaches for her. You remember being told how Ruby died of scarlet fever. I made her casket, Mother lined it with pretty cloth. It hurt her bad to see me and a friend put that little girl on a sled, go across the ice to Whitefish Point and bury her in House's cemetery. I left the service for a while to try homesteading. Mother loved it. She had a garden and I was home. She didn't have to worry about me drowning some place. Then we burned out. I tried working at Edison in Detroit but Mother could see I wasn't happy. I wanted to get back in the Service. I signed up in the Lighthouse Service, served at Detroit River Light until I was transferred to Devil's Island in Wisconsin. That was hard on her, too, moving back and forth from the Island to Bayfield twice a year. When you were born there I almost lost her. She had a real hard time." Dad's voice held such sadness I wished he'd stop talking. I was feeling guilty about it all.

"Big Bay Light wasn't too bad. There were other fami-lies. We weren't there long. You were about a year old when I transferred to Stannard Rock. She was alone a lot raising you kids. Mother's life hasn't been easy. She wants to try it at Newberry. Aunt Gert (Mother's sister) is there. We're going to try farming. Chickens, a cow, maybe, and a garden. You'll enjoy it once you get there."

Hearing a person's life was like being on a roller coaster. Life was good, life was bad. Rebellion gave way to sympathy. I knew Dad wouldn't be happy away from the lake. How could he? His life had been spent in service to others on the Lakes. But if he wanted to try it at Newberry, I'd have to go. There was no other way.

"Do you think we could have a horse, Dad?"

"You bet! Let's get in out of this cold."

chapter

22

Saying Goodbye

Time was marching on. Emmett was home to help in getting the Newberry property ready for us. Each day Dad was free we traveled to Newberry to clear land for a house. Dad was not a carpenter so the going was slow. He had Uncle Tony to help which was a good thing. Mother, Theresa, Wayne, Carol and I dug great clumps of grass and weeds for the garden spot Mom was eager to plant. We heard the thump of the big block of wood, dropped from a scaffold onto a pipe being driven into the ground, which turned out to be an artesian well of water so cold I could barely drink it.

I missed Whitefish whenever we were away. Life would not be the same. Realizing my childhood was gone tore at me. I imagined myself growing up, getting married, and having children who would love life at Whitefish as I did. Even as the dream continued I knew it would never be. I tried hard to accept what I could not change.

The Robinsons, the second assistant's family, were the first to leave. I heard he was in the Coast Guard now. The Captain's family were packing. I didn't know where they were going. I spent most of my free time at the lakeshore. Searching for agates, skipping rocks across the smooth water, or making castles in the sand, helped me hold on to life as I had become accustomed to.

The day finally came. All the packing was done. Dad was officially out of the service.

"We'll leave in the morning, so say your goodbyes to this place," Dad said.

"We'll come back for visits once in a while," Mom tried to console us.

I ran from the house wanting to say goodbye all by myself. As I went from one special place to another I recognized a difference in myself. Maybe the changes I faced over the past year had made me grow up a little. Soon I would be in my teens. A new school, a new life, might not be so bad after all. My childhood at Whitefish Point would always be a part of me. I could always escape to the sand dunes or lakeshore in my imagination. I finished my goodbyes, turned toward the house we would soon be leaving, and joined my family.

23

Dad's Special Gift

Dad took hold of my arm. "Come with me," he said. What did I do now? I asked myself. He led the way up the stairway to the door to the walkway leading to the light tower. Excitement burst like a punctured water balloon in my heart. The steps, I was so excited I forgot to count, wound around and around until a door was opened above our heads. Dad helped me out, around the magnificent light, onto the outside walkway around the tower. I was in the sky! The deep blue of Lake Superior spread before us like a giant blanket covering the earth.

"Oh! Dad, Oh! Dad," was all I could say. Many times I dreamed about standing out here in all kinds of weather. Today was the perfect day. A thousand whitecaps danced over the surface of the dark blue water, as if they had come out to say goodbye to me. Sea gulls screamed as they swooped riding the breeze. Letting go of the rail. I stood allowing the beauty of Dad's special gift enfold me.

"Time to go, Sis." Dad touched my arm.

We climbed down all the stairs until we stood in the front room Dad had used for his office. His roll top desk and everything else was gone. Somehow it seemed all right. All my daydreams of Whitefish Point were no longer daydreams, but memories. I'd take them with me wherever I'd go.

"Thanks Dad," I said. His smile and wink told me he understood.

Vivian DeRusha Quantz

Epilogue

Several times over the ensuing years, while visiting my parent's graves in the Whitefish Point Cemetery, I was saddened to see the deterioration of the Whitefish Point Light Station. The buildings became rundown, the light tower lost it's crisp white look, the grounds became overgrown and uncared for. The old schoolhouse became more and more ramshackled and finally disappeared altogether.

Trying to convey to my children what a great childhood I spent at Whitefish Point was difficult when my heart was heavy upon seeing the condition of that wonderful place.

In September of 1988, after having had a disabling electric shock, I returned to the lighthouse trying desperately to revive my damaged memory. I had the opportunity to speak with Tom Farnquist, Director of the Great Lakes Shipwreck Historical Society of Sault Ste. Marie and Whitefish Point, Michigan. Encouraged by the restoration efforts of my beloved light station, and prompted by Tom's questions, the restoration of my memories began.

Seeing the Shipwreck Museum for the first time reminded me of the many storms experienced at the Point, and the concern and attention the light keepers showed for the ships that passed, especially when bad weather posed a risk. My father spent those times at the fog signal building and watching the light to make sure they kept sending life saving messages throughout the storms.

The Birds of Prey Exhibit was especially interesting to me having been frightened by a hawk many years before. A special treat was meeting with Avis and Phyllis Hutton and Dick Rikard after so many years, at the Dedication of Quarters.

These memories have been written to impart some of this history to those who will never have the experience as lighthouse keepers and their families.

Returning to the Upper Peninsula in 1988 caused more excitement when I became a member of the Sault Ste. Marie Tribe of Chippewa Indians. After so many years of knowing my Indian ancestry, becoming a member of the Tribe gave me great pleasure.

In 1996 Howard and I bought a piece of property in Skandia, Michigan, and became residents once again, getting reacquainted with relatives and renewing old friendships.

The property has an abandoned portion of old U.S. Highway 41 running through it with woods all around. Deer, rabbits, squirrels, porcupines, raccoons, partridge and an occasional harrier hawk, feed while we have the pleasure of watching. Our latest visitor, a black bear, empties the corn feeder quickly, and a black and white heifer, from a nearby farm, found it's way to the road one day. For-get-me Knots and Swamp Roses turn the sides of the road into blankets of blue and gold. Howard spends his time clearing brush and cutting wood, while in the quietness, I put my memories on paper.

Dad and Jeanette with car
that brought family to
Devil's Island, Wisconsin

Dad, Emmett and Vivian at
Big Bay, Michigan

Vivian and Theresa, corner
of Michigan & Pine Streets
Marquette, Michigan

Teddy and Bobby on wharf
at Whitefish Point

Home at Big Bay, Michigan
Light Station 1930

Mr. Cools, Captain Wilkes
and Dad at Stannard Rock
Lighthouse, Lake Superior

Aunt Jane Goudreau
St. Ignace, Michigan

U.S. Coast Guard Vermillion Life Saving Station Early 1900's

Captain Christianson and First Asst. Louis C. DeRusha

Devil's Island Lighthouse, Bayfield Wisconsin
Photo by Faystrom Photo, Eau Claire, Wisconsin

Big Bay Lighthouse
Photo by Emerson & Linda Fleury
Big Bay, Michigan

Dad and Emmett at Big Bay

Stannard Rock Lighthouse

Dad on Lighthouse boat.
Ready to go to the "ROCK"

Dad, 2nd Asst. Sormunen, Capt. Wilkes
Kitchen Band heard over short wave radio from the "ROCK"